Dedication

I dedicate this chapbook to every soul whose voice has been silenced, every voice that has gone unheard, and to voices trapped in fear.

Introduction

This collection of poems was inspired by much of what is going on in the world. In our human experience, we encounter an enormous amount of social injustice, domestic violence, and other things that eat at our humanity. It appears to be deterioration in our quality of life, which I think affects our diligence in being socially responsible. My sincere hope is that these poems awaken something in you so that you make personal changes, whether it be attitude or behavior, and that it will spark a light in others, and one by one we begin to change our world.

"Be the change that you wish to see in the world." – Mahatma Gandhi

Table of Contents

Watts

I'm screaming bloody murder.

I'm crying searing tears.

I'm running with all my might

Yet our plight goes unheard,

Our tears untouched,

Our screams silenced.

We are chased,

We are beaten,

We are accused,

Constantly abused by this system.

They don't understand our unrest,

Look surprised when we respond with violent protest.

I'm screaming bloody murder.

I'm crying searing tears.

I'm running with all my might,

Running frantically for my life.

Press

Opposition presses hard against our backs,

Desiring to see us fall, never to rise.

Uncertainty lies before us

But we can only move forward.

Hand in hand, shoulder to shoulder,

We must stand united.

We must be an unbreakable chain,

Never to rust,

Never to lose purpose.

Together we are stronger.

Our lives depend on each other.

We are sisters and brothers

In a strange land, eating strange food.

But we're here.

Nourish one another with love and tolerance.

Feed each other with knowledge and wisdom.

We are our only survival, we are our only escape.

Let's step up to the plate.

Let's plow through these gates of hate and injustice.

Let's overturn every refuge of lies that have stifled our growth,

Kept us imprisoned in our minds.

We were born free

And no man can hinder.

Let us open our eyes and remember...

We are gods.

If I Were An Immigrant

My mama said we came here for freedom

She wanted me to attend better schools

Grow up and have better job

But people here

They treat me different

Guess cause of fear

Or maybe anger

We just wanted to escape the dangers of my country

But we get treated like fleas

Annoying pests

And all I want is to be my best

An American

So I speak English even though it's broken

Hoping I will be accepted

I pretend I can read and that I don't need help

That I can handle everything by myself

If they only knew where I came from

Dirt floors

Bathrooms outdoors

My chores were standing on corners selling, begging

Mama tried to give us a slice of heaven

Make us like unleavened bread

Instead we are fed to those who hate what they don't know

They don't like me cause I'm Brown

Not white like snow

Aftermath

Rioting in the minds of the benevolent,

war never ceasing

because there is no justice,

no peace in the land of the exploited,

home of the cowards.

Fragile lives valued at zero.

Indignation stifled by lies about equity.

Stars that once illuminated the sky are fallen, forgotten.

God bear us in the arms of love, truth, and mercy.

Watchful Eyes

Their eyes watched God as they were sold into slavery.

Their eyes watched God as they were dehumanized on ships.

Their eyes watched God as they were beaten, murdered, separated, merchandized.

Their eyes watched God as they were raped, left for dead, stripped of everything except their soul.

Their eyes watched God but was it too late?

Was it something their ancestors did that brought this fate?

Was God angry with the children who had melanin in their skin?

What was the sin they committed worthy of this punishment?

I'm sure those were the questions behind their eyes

When they looked up into blood filled skies

Raining injustice and cruelty.

Over 300 years of suffering and woe,

Tears, terror, taunts daily prescribed

Yet by some miracle their spirits survived.

Broken but not destroyed,

Their glory remained alive.

Though it seemed God was silent,

Their stares he must have caught.

Secretly he raised up heroic, valiant men and women who loved more than most

Loved sacrificially, prized justice and liberty,

Whose souls wouldn't rest until they tasted victory.

And it was bitter sweet.

But once they broke forth they saw they had potential to lead,

Limits could be pushed and foundations shaken.

Discovered truth and no one can take it.

Freedom Writers

Writing with purpose.

Writing for their lives.

Writing under the weight of oppression,

Pen speaking up for human rights—deprived.

Reminding we are all created equal,

Same blood running through veins.

None inferior.

All created with intellectual capabilities,

None fit for enslavement.

Who really acted like cave men?

Yeah, the real barbarians—

The ones who sexually exploited mothers and daughters.

The real animals—

The ones who murdered and slaughtered.

Freedom writers were born despite illiteracy;

They pursued education, liberty, independence to tell a story.

Slave narratives and poems to give accounts of savagery,

A cry to abolish an abominable institution.

They bled ink in the name of restitution.

Response to "I Have A Dream" Speech

Dr. King, reminded America that 100 years after the Emancipation Proclamation,

We still had mountains to climb.

My heart is vexed to see 51 years later,

Many of us are still plagued, still not free,

Crippled, blatantly discriminated against,

Still stranded on the island of poverty.

Yes, our discontent is warranted,

But when will we rise up

And get ourselves out of the pit?

We can't sit here until we die.

We can't be complacent with integration,

We can't fall into this slumber,

Lulled by entertainment,

Overindulgent in physical pleasure.

What are we doing for each other?

What are we doing to break vicious cycles?

What are we doing to destroy curses?

Have we lost sight of our true enemy?

No one can stop us

But we must believe in ourselves,

See beyond the veil of oppression,

Frame our own worlds

With our thoughts and words.

Build on a strong foundation

And through walking in love and truth

Reshape this nation.

Return

Beginning to think maybe just maybe we are perpetuating a defeatist attitude

By being glued to images that only reflect horror, shame, and degradation,

Sprinkled with a little pseudo freedom.

Maybe just maybe the purpose has gotten lost

Or the message was blurred all along

Sending subliminal messages wrapped in freedom songs.

Replay the tape and it says "we" hate you, hate yourselves.

We abolished slavery on paper

But paper trail still leading back to slave owners

Just different names, same faces, a little more cunning.

When will we become wiser?

We need to know the story before the Middle Passage,

Who we were in the ancient land.

Power in Darkness

They didn't want us to see,

Why the separated us.

Our identity crucified on many trees.

Awakening is overdue.

We must search for the truth,

Remember from where we were taken,

Forsaking everything that does not empower,

Clutching all that renews.

Mass Graves

Buried with no dignity

No shred of decency

Compiled in the dirt

In which we're all destined to return

But not like this

Victims ripped from life

Tossed like garbage

How far is the oppressor willing to go

Casualties of war

Casualties of genocide

Casualties of being something other than...

Ashes to ashes

Dust to dust

Slain

Left to rot

Villainy without a thought

Bloody hands stay unclean

Wickedness flows like a stream

Innocent screams fall on deaf ears

Rivers of tears stopped by the damned

But the righteous souls will rise

And their lights will shine

Bursting out of obscurity

Famished

Hungry for death,

Ruthless vulture breathes down the baby's neck.

Hungry for life,

Helpless baby holds on to his last breath.

Will night fall before he finds strength,

Or sustenance to move on,

Or will he become a predator's feast?

What I don't understand is how ends don't meet,

How we can eat comfortably

While children die in the streets.

This is one out of millions that stare death in the face,

Not flavorful food but poverty they taste.

Bitter gall in their tummies

While Fat Cats have surplus.

These facts and these numbers just don't add up.

The earth that we live in produces enough.

So tell me why millions are starving,

Vulnerable bodies falling victim to illness...

All because capitalism is big business.

Unequal distribution

Is the pollution,

The root,

That silent killer,

The vulture

That preys on the poor.

Media Frenzy

Weezy said it best,

"Women lie, men lie, Women lie, men lie,

Women lie, men lie, Numbers don't lie."

Yet the media would have us deceived

Brainwashing us to believe propaganda

Pumping images of violence at every turn

Flashing horrors with every blink

The people sink into fear

Ready to surrender rights in the fight against terror

To run when no one is chasing

Contrary to popular belief

Gun violence is down

Way less than 2 decades ago

Say it ain't so

Yes, as a matter of fact

Firearm homicides plummeted

Assaults, robberies, and sex crimes also took a dive

So what's all this jive talk?

Making people afraid to walk around the city

Let's get down to the nitty gritty

Reporters got us thinking gun crime is higher

While numbers tell a different story

Meanwhile the ones telling us we don't need guns for safety

Have guns protecting them

Why should we be left defenseless?

Where I'm from police are useless

They don't exercise their authority until somebody's dead

By then it's way too late

That's another debate

The question at hand is

Why all the media frenzy

Beckoning us to believe times are worse than they really are?

Ain't nobody saying nothing but...

Um...control

Best way to control the masses is through fear

Let's get them to shed tears over mirages, allusions

Political contusions

Abusing their power to gain even more

The truth is, steel is not the enemy

Weapons are not as deadly as corruption

Pure freedom has already been massacred

American dream deferred for many

While Fat Cats eating good and plenty

Shh!

Society has the tendency to want to silence us

Begging us to hush and stay quiet

Afraid we might riot

Against social injustice

Corporate corruption

Blatant racism

Schisms in religion

Impotent politics

If sticks and stones break bones

But words don't hurt

Why must my mouth stay closed

I have the right to expose deception

I have the right to tell my story

It's within bounds to inquire

About things that confound me

It's astounding you wish to keep my lips locked

I've been quiet for too long

Accepting wrong for right

But I'm not a child of the night

My aura is too bright

Gifted with spiritual sight

It's time for me to fight

Even if you pin my lips

I dip my pen in ink

And it will speak for me

Long after I'm gone

My imprint will remain

Changing frames of mind

Beckoning the next star to shine

Cyberbullying

Cowards behind computers

Taking cheap shots

Spouting obscenities

Striking deafening blows

While no one knows the depth of wounds

Children dying too soon

Thinking they're unworthy

Digital blood spilling

Words killing

Cyber space... verbal assassinations...

The worst cases

Dark Blue

When I see blue and white

And red flashing lights,

My first instinct is to run...

Not because I'm guilty

But because you mean me harm.

Embossed on your badge is protect and serve

Yet when you stop and frisk me

There is no justice heard,

Just racial slurs and profanities

And my chest hitting the concrete.

My only crime is having skin of color.

I was adjusting my waistband,

You said I made furtive movements,

If I blink too hard

You'll be ready to shoot me.

You call it proactive policing

But we know the truth.

You are the thieves that are robbing our youth

Of dignity and pride,

Forced to take racial profiling in stride.

You say it's for my own safety,

Well you can keep those lies.

If that were true, unarmed kids wouldn't die

At your hand

By your cops.

Let us stop and frisk you.

I know what we'd find,

A zeal to lock up all coloreds,

Make 'em all do time.

We'd find a seared conscience, unable to feel.

Think you deserve honor,

You're just keeping it real.

Real foul,

Real corrupt.

We won't bow down,

We will continue to speak up

Against your policies,

Against your fraud,

Against your prejudice that you call Law.

Overdue

I bore your sons

But when the sun goes down

You want to fight me in the night

See you won't do it in front of the kids

But who are we kidding

I've stood by your side

15 years as your wife

But you've come within inches of taking my life

You say you don't remember

That you were drunk

Is that supposed to give me comfort

I love, you hurt

You don't see me for what I'm worth

If I don't leave now I'll be buried in dirt

This'll be the last time you pull a gun

It's been a long time coming

I am done

She Doesn't See Me

She doesn't see me at all

I remind her too much of my father

She thinks I will end up lost like my brother

Maybe she doesn't see me because she'll see her failures as a mother

She doesn't see me, no not at all

Ever since my father left

She's built this wall

Seems the only way through is to claw my way in

But will she forgive me for my dad's sins

She's made the couch her home

The TV's her companion

I sometimes leave her sandwiches and a cool drink

Just to let her know I'm thinking of her

Still love her... even though she doesn't see me

I run these streets to make bread

I know Momma thinks I'll end up dead

But I'm fed up with this system

That doesn't listen to the blood in the streets

Designed to keep us pacified

What's the point of being alive

If all we do is struggle to survive

Since Momma don't see me

Maybe I'll shrink back into the darkness

Become heartless

Avenge myself and reap a harvest.

Broken Promises

The boy is growing up

into a young man.

His eyes are open,

his mind is aware

that something is missing,

someone is missing.

Anger, resentment bubble beneath his skin.

If not careful, he will erupt.

What is he realizing?

The sun has no heaven,

the heaven has no stars?

He is disconnected from his earth.

He is alone in the galaxy.

He doesn't see his reflection.

He yearns for attention, affection

but all he gets are broken promises.

Nothing is his gift.

Abandonment is his friend.

Taken

Carefree

This girl

Innocent and naïve.

She flowed with the breeze

Her heart skipping beats

As she followed her dreams.

She was in her own lane

When dogs jumped in the road,

Grabbed her legs and attacked

Mauling and groping

Assaulting her flesh.

Tearing her virtue to pieces

Sucking her life out like leeches.

They left her a shadow

Her light had gone out.

Her world was overcast with fear and doubt.

How could this happen?

Who was to blame?

Could she recover? Could she be the same?

The police never found her rapists' names.

Scarred

This girl

Defiled and abused

She hides among the trees.

Her mind playing tricks

As she struggles to sleep.

Deflowered

His hands deep in my pockets

As if he's searching for dimes

But I have no change.

Yet this strange man's fingers linger in my pockets.

I'm sure I should stop him but I don't.

Stupefied and shocked,

I let him pry in my pants

Foraging for a flower not in bloom.

I suppose he assumed I liked it

Because I didn't move,

My grandma in the same room.

How come she didn't see

The panic in my face,

Didn't hear my silent screams?

I sometimes think it was a dream

But it was a nightmare

And when I told her shortly after...

She didn't care.

Thief

He forced seed down her throat

Commanded her not to choke.

Her arm violently broke

When she tried to get away.

It all happened so fast

Sleeping soundly

Awakened by a CRASH

Door knocked off hinges.

Before she could think, he was at her bed

She slunk under the covers, gun to her head.

All she could think was she didn't want to end up dead.

At first she tried to comply

Simply wanted to survive

This night of torment, home invasion

Robbed of peace and security.

She would bleed long after this.

He took his time

His words made no sense

He spoke like he knew her and maybe he did

His face she never saw

He took advantage of her like he was above the law.

The moment she tried to fight

He overpowered her with all his might.

He was gross darkness that came to steal her light.

He left her broken

Void of life.

Marred

Her cut wrists left her bloody joy

Many years of pain she wanted to drain

She dreamt of sun but only rain came

She wanted to recover but nothing was the same

She walked invisible; she desired fame

Given an impossible hand; she hated the game

She sacrificed but no one knew her name

Feeling hopeless and useless

She wanted control

Just to feel relief, she'd sell her soul

Void too big, nothing filled the hole

Took a knife to her strife

Used her power to end ...life

200 Cries

Over 200 Nigerian girls stolen

My heart is swollen with hurt

Wondering how on earth these tragedies happen

Extremist rebels fascinated by the fear they incite

While they go and recite prayers

At peace with crushing hearts into pieces

What species is this that abducts young women...

Punishing who for what sins...

Nobody wins in this war

I can't wrap my mind around violence

Why governments are silent

Massive explosions

Human lives lost

What will it cost to redeem our souls?

Bold enemies in all forms are vigilant

But citizens are not supposed to become militant

"They" don't want us to bear arms

Even though the alarm is sounding

We are surrounded by so much hate

In the name of Love and God

But innocence and purity have been robbed

Civilization is imploding

No one is voting for deconstruction or revolution

Blood cries out from North, South, East, and West for a solution

We can't see for all the pollution

Still enslaved with invisible nooses

How am I supposed to process this nonsense?

In our bubbles we think we're safe

While teenage girls are being raped

Untold abuse their fate

Soon this story will be out of date

If we don't wake up, it will be too late

Are our hearts too cold, our consciences already seared

That we don't grieve for problems that aren't near?

No one is exempt

In the court of compassion, we are in contempt

What affects one affects us all

But our vision is so small

We look no further than an arm's stretch

Until our own is wrapped in death

I just had to get this out

Couldn't hold my breath

Reform

What is it like being locked away for five years

Nothing but time to sit and face all your fears

Did your offense match the consequence

Who am I to say

But I admire you for keeping hope each day

Seems to me you've paid a great price

Stolen moments of your life

The system says they believe in rehabilitation

If that were true

Why are you still incarcerated

I don't know what else they want you to prove

Gone before the parole board and each time you lose

I believe you have repented

Yet they want to maximize your sentence

Did they take into account your state of mind

Or were you just a pay check

To your hurt they were blind

No second chances for black single mothers

Might as well been a part of a coven

Took one look and called you evil

But they are the ones... unmerciful people

I still stand in agreement for your release

Praying always for your peace

And that your soul will find relief.

Listen

Listen...

Has the heart of hip hop stopped beating

Listen...

Air waves crowded with music lacking meaning

The one universal language we have

defiled by lethal lyrics

Opening a gateway to harmful and foul spirits

You don't have to take my word

Just listen...

First skittles, you might know it as ex was on the scene

Now it's popping mollies

If you know what I mean

Don't forget about blowing that smoke

Sipping that syrup

And snorting that coke

Come down with some xanis

Or whatever your choice

Is this the way we choose to use our voice

What's getting high gon' do for us

Get faded faded for what

So we can keep getting screwed

Singing the blues

And how we can't seem to stop losing

The very things we listen to are choking hope

It's a time and a place for partying

But what are we really celebrating

If all we're trying to do is not remember

Chasing highs but feeling low

How far in the darkness must we go

So deep in slumber

Not even Thunder awakens us

If lighting strikes would it move us

Or would we say it won't strike the same place twice

We embrace death instead of life

Following strange Voices on the mic

Oh it's a club banger, don't get all deep

Bobbing your head but you are asleep

Unconscious of subliminal messages

Glorifying that which destroys our communities

Addiction, jail, and STDs...a result of these...

These misguided exploits of trapping,

sexing, and getting loaded

And the truth is we just can't afford it

Listen... the cost is too great

We have too much at stake

To be raped by a culture

That demeans who we are

We must look within for the stars

I'm crying, I'm crying, crying in the streets

Just listen...

Please take heed

What I'm giving you is meat

Chew on it...I know it's not sweet

But it's truth I'm feeding you

I urge you to eat.

With Love, Earth

I was put into this universe to foster life

The Creator made me with land and trees

Oceans and seas

Spectacular things

But see I'm not just to nurture you

We are to nurture each other

A partnership is most fitting

But humans always seem to be sitting

Too high on a throne

To recognize their own error

So I make no apologies for the terror my superstorms bring

You don't listen when the birds sing

What baffles me is this...

Even in the grips of death

You continue to test me

With depleting my ozone

Polluting my water

Degrading everything I stand for...

Yet you want more...

If you don't heed my warnings

And embrace me with love

More than acid rain will come from above

You'll keep your skin cancer

And your newborns defective

Stop burying the truth like no one suspects it's you

Killing me slowly

Realize that it's suicide

Because if there's no me, there's no you

It's not a threat, it's true

I react this way because I love you

People say I'm bipolar

And maybe I am

But there must be balance between you and I

Live harmoniously and consciously with me

Be my eco lover

Civil Unrest

What is the solution

To political pollution

Vile corruption

Racial oppression

We need more than confessions

Less institutions

They are useless

Minds prostituted for filthy lucre

But no one really wants to stir the pot

Because the ones who do typically get shot

Silenced or buried one way or another

When will we realize we all need each other

To survive and stay alive

We must let go of fear and pride

Wide is the grave made for those who won't think for themselves

Who drink from the well of mediocrity

People too busy arguing philosophies

But all these degrees ain't got us free

I'm not just talking about one color

I speak of humanity

The ones whose hearts bleed

Enslaved to poverty

The working poor

Leaves once green falling from trees

Believing in liberty, "we" vote

But are the people heard

Excuse me if I step on toes

But I see nothing more than an illusion

A false impression

To keep us wishing with worthless pennies

Into a fountain of lies

Our greatest leaders have died

Who dared reveal the truth

What blazing torch will we pass our youth

As my eyes continue to open

And I see what's what

I know why revolution is the only solution

If we want radical change

We must be the change.

Uprising

From the ashes

From the muck

The oppressed look up and within

Ready to defend their freedom

Being dead already, they have nothing to lose

Everything to prove to themselves

That they aren't merely pawns

Groping in darkness

Waiting for Dawn

No, now they stand

Ready to fight

With all their might

Refusing to buckle and cave

Rebuking the mentality of slaves

Waxing brave

In the face of evil

The will to live has grown stronger

No longer satisfied with status quo

Wanting more out of life

More to give to their seed

Wanting to breathe deep

To sleep in peace

Live their dreams out loud

Reach higher than the clouds

What they found was purpose

Pain unearthed it

Only courage will birth it

Truth

What if the truth we learned was not truth at all?

What if truth was dressed in allusion, analogy?

What if what you believed to be true

Was man personifying deity?

Is partial truth still truth or does it become a lie?

What if truth is all based on interpretation, human perception?

Could you recognize the truth if it came to you?

Would you think truth was a lie?

Could you really handle THE truth?

What is the truth but what we choose to believe?

What is truth but lessons experience has taught us?

What is truth but our own conscience?

Nude

What if we were all naked?

What if we could not hide behind suits and ties?

What if we couldn't overcompensate with tight dresses and pretty blouses

And everyone saw us for who we really are?

Stripped of all fallacies and illusions

Completely undisguised

No room for lies to hide.

I mean what are we afraid of?

What are we so desperately trying to cover?

The ugliness of our spirit

The greediness of our souls

Insecurity

Fear

Self- loathing...

If we were all exposed

Maybe there would be more humility

Maybe we would see we're all fragile

All...vulnerable

All...human.

We need to cast away garments of hate

Cast off garments of pride

Cast off garments of selfishness.

We are a many membered body in grave need of a revolution on every scale

From politics to our own personalities.

We came here naked

Born to be open

No need for protection or shield

No need to be concealed.

Will we return to the day of no shame

Of no wars in the name of peace...

To the days hearts can be naked and free...

Civilized

We say we are civilized

Yet we dehumanize each other

Behave like savages

We put bandages over putrid wounds

Spoon feed hate to babies

Parade around like gents and ladies

But underneath is far less noble

We have a global epidemic

It all boils down to power and control

The haves making have nots fold

The stories that matter go untold

People with hearts of gold are martyred

Daring to dive in waters unchartered

When will we stop being driven by fear

Start being driven by love

When will we begin to think for ourselves

And yet respect our differences

Divisions are hindrances

Which leaves us on the hinges of discord

And can we afford to be out of sync

Can we not find one thing to link us

If what we have now is civilized

There is much more to be realized

If I were Madam President

I would make sure time was spent

Overhauling our entire government system

No more working poor

Fat Cats getting rich off the backs of them

Who are enslaved to the clock

I would put a stop to ludicrous CEO bonus checks

I would evenly spread the wealth

And demand companies compensate men and women what they're worth

As for our education system

This No Child Left Behind

Kids still falling through the cracks

I've had about enough of that

Our schools will no longer teach to the test

But they will differentiate instruction

And take children out of boxes

They need to have choices

They have the right to express their voices

Yes we need to build them up

Science, Mathematics, Engineering

And room still must be made for the Arts

Communities must play a part

All this misappropriating of funds

Superintendents and higher ups running away with money

Meant to provide technology and resources for our kids

Well I'm getting rid of you

And you're serving hard time

For taking the shine out of innocent eyes

America, I'm a firm believer in taking care of home first

We don't need to look far for thirsty and hungry souls

And don't worry about jumping in other people's affairs

We have our own terrorist scares

They don't come from guns and bombs

So we won't be fighting other countries' wars

We'll be opening doors of opportunity

Living out what it truly means to be free

I'm shutting down conspiracies

Slaying the beast

So this land and its people can experience real peace

No Covert ops, no secret societies

So the mind of the people can be at ease

I'll provide relief to those that need it

Securing jobs for those that seek them

Banning outsourcing

I'm for people not just profit

And I will veto every bill that tries to stop it

There is so much I could get into

Just know that I'm here for YOU

I will not be a puppet

Or Miss Mary on a tuffet eating curds and whey

But I will make every criminal pay restitution

And I ain't talking about those in institutions

But the ones in suits walking free

They won't believe it was little ole me

Made 'em walk the Green Mile

Serving justice with a smile

www.ingramcontent.com/pod-product-compliance
Lightning Source LLC
Chambersburg PA
CBHW070228290526
45789CB00004B/1537